Mommy

LAWYER

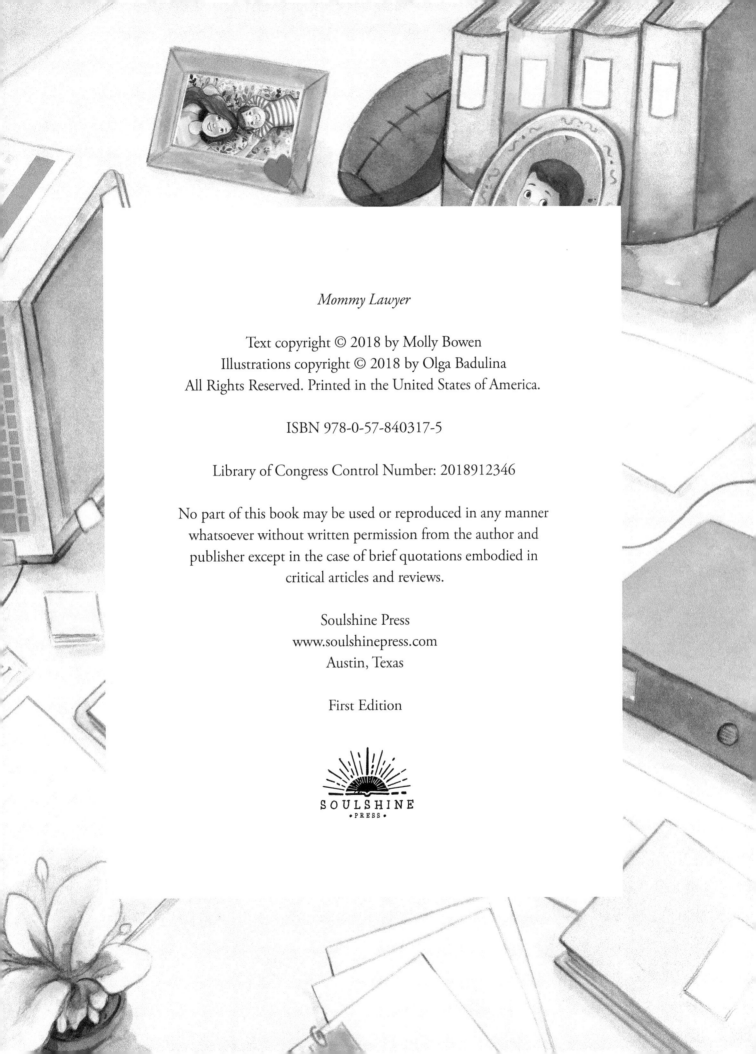

Mommy Lawyer

Text copyright © 2018 by Molly Bowen
Illustrations copyright © 2018 by Olga Badulina
All Rights Reserved. Printed in the United States of America.

ISBN 978-0-57-840317-5

Library of Congress Control Number: 2018912346

Soulshine Press
www.soulshinepress.com
Austin, Texas

First Edition

SOULSHINE
• PRESS •

For my husband Micah and our boys Sam, Sawyer & Finn—thank you for loving me through the chaos, for supporting my wild dreams, and for never asking me to choose.

For my mentor Amber Mostyn, the greatest mommy lawyer of all—thank you for pushing me forward and believing in me (no matter how many times I went on maternity leave).

And for every other mommy lawyer doing it all— this is for you.

Mommy
LAWYER

by Molly Bowen

illustrated by Olga Badulina

Soulshine Press, LLC

Being a mom is one big job to do.
But, believe it or not, my mom has two!

My mom is a mom – that's her job number one.
And clearly that job is the one that's most fun!

Mom's second job is called being a lawyer.
And, boy, does she have a demanding employer!

Mom studied extra hard while she was in school
and read lots of books and learned lots of rules.

Then she aced all her tests
and launched her career.

Now she solves problems
every day of the year!

Most lawyers work on cases and there's always two sides.

If two people can't agree, then
a judge or jury decides.

Some lawyers stop bad guys from breaking our laws.
Other lawyers help people fight for a cause.

Like making sure businesses treat their employees fair or stopping a company from polluting our air.

Lawyers can help families to adopt a child
or ensure that your taxes are properly filed.

A lawyer's work isn't easy –
it can be rather tough.

But people are counting
on them to do really big stuff.

Having two jobs can keep
Mom super busy.

Her jam-packed agenda
makes most people dizzy.

Sometimes Mom gets dressed in her suit and high heels

and goes to big meetings and closes big deals.

Sometimes she works hard
at her desk all day
when I know she'd rather
come out and play.

And sometimes she needs help
from a jury or judge
to solve a big case when
the other side won't budge.

Usually she wins,
but sometimes she loses.
It depends on which side the
jury chooses.

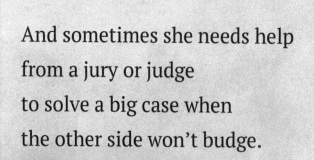

But Mom fights for what's right,
and she stands up for what's true

making the world a better place
for me and for you.

She might miss a class party
or skip field day,
but lawyers have deadlines
and court orders to obey!

I try not to be sad if Mom misses something fun.
She rushes straight home to me when her work is all done.

Mom always makes time
for the things that matter most.

Like bedtime stories, bike rides, and
homemade French toast.

So, if you have a mom that's a lawyer too...
Be proud of your mom! She's working hard for you!

And remember, having
two jobs isn't easy to do.

so give her a big hug
and some extra I love yous!

ABOUT THE AUTHOR

MOLLY BOWEN practices law and writes books in Wimberley, Texas while farmsteading with her husband and three sons. She wrote her first book *Mommy Lawyer* to teach her children about her career but, more importantly, to give herself and other mommy lawyers a tool to help teach young children to be more understanding, supportive, and proud of their working mother.

Molly knows firsthand the challenges working mothers face when trying to balance both career and motherhood. She took the bar exam nine months pregnant with her first child. A few days later, her son was born, and Molly landed a job at a fast-pace litigation firm. Two more baby boys followed, and, within three years, Molly was juggling a heavy caseload at work and three little boys at home.

After taking the time to teach her children about her career through *Mommy Lawyer*, Molly discovered her children were less disappointed and more understanding when she occasionally missed a special day at school or didn't make it home in time to tuck them in. While we may never fully eliminate "mommy guilt," Molly hopes this book will help children see their working mother's career in a more positive light.

Mommy Lawyer is the first of a series of children's books dedicated to developing a more compassionate and supportive relationship between working parents and their children. Learn more at mollybowen.com.

ABOUT THE ILLUSTRATOR

OLGA BADULINA is an international illustrator living in Finland with her husband and two children. Olga received a bachelor of arts with an emphasis in painting from Novgorod State University in Saint Petersburg, Russia in 2001.

Olga draws inspiration from everything around her—whether it's the animals she finds walking through the forest or old architecture on a bustling city street. Olga loves capturing every nuance and texture using her favorite medium, watercolors. Olga's art is featured in many delightful children's books around the globe, and she has worked with authors throughout the United States, Russia, Europe, and Australia. Readers can view more of her art at olyabad.com.

CPSIA information can be obtained
at www.ICGtesting.com
Printed in the USA
BVHW010959051219
565405BV00054BA/51/P